YOUR LEADS WON'T CALL THEMSELVES

A FOLLOWUP TO THE *Timeless* SELF-HELP BOOK: *CALL YOUR LEADS*

CLAY CLARK & STEVE "THE LAMBORGHINI-DRIVING MORTGAGE LENDER" CURRINGTON

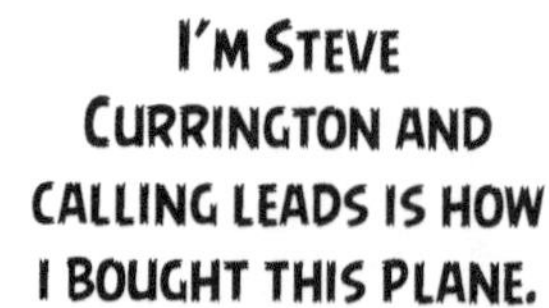

Steve Currington

Pictured above is a plane/Lamborghini combo pack that Steve has purchased by calling his leads.

Your Leads Won't Call Themselves
ISBN 979-8-9864278-9-8
Copyright 2023 by Clay Clark

Published by Clay Clark Publishing
3920 West 91st Street South
Tulsa, OK 74132

Printed in the United States of America.
All rights reserved.

Any part of this book may be used or reproduced
in any manner whatsoever without written
permission. For information text Clay Clark at:
918-851-0102

Clay Clark Publishing books may be purchased
for educational, business, or sales promotional
use at: www.ThrivetimeShow.com

I'm Steve Currington and I follow-up with my staff 8 times per day to call their leads.
LAMBROS

I'm Steve Currington and I endorse calling your leads.

HOW TO USE THIS BOOK:

Sales managers, call center managers, business owners, business leaders, organization leaders, and marketing managers for years have been puzzled, befuddled, and confused as to why their sales people will not call their leads. So elaborate sales funnels, customer relationship management software, and team management software has been created in an attempt to motivate, to stimulate, to educate, and irritate salespeople into actually calling their leads. A team member may be the best closer in the world, but picking up the phone and dialing the phone seems to be nearly impossible for many people. Are sales calls not being placed by salespeople because they are afraid of making calls were because they don't know what leads to call? Because of the fear of rejection or because a still small voice in their cranium is telling them not to make calls? Is mere laziness to blame? Is too much soy being consumed in the standard American diet? Is the great cosmic wealth repulsion system and universal habit force known as "Jackassery" to blame? Are there not enough sales books and self-help books in circulation about the art of sales, selling things, and making sales calls?

In this book, I attempt to stop the poverty being caused by poor performing sales people living and working in your office by providing YOU and YOUR TEAM with 101 practical sales tips and SUPER MOVES that you can use to dramatically improve your team's sales performance. You must use this book as a guidebook, as a sales compass, and as if your sales, your income, and family's level of wealth depends on it.

"But if any provide not for his own, and specially for those of his own house, he hath denied the faith, and is worse than an infidel."
- I Timothy 5:8

"People often say that motivation doesn't last. Well, neither does bathing, that's why we recommend it daily."

- Zig Ziglar

(The best-selling author and legendary motivational speaker and traine.r)

If you know of anyone in your life or in your office that needs these incredibly deep and wealth increasing sales book, feel free to buy another copy of this book (which is not free). My sincere desire is that this book will help both you and your team to move beyond Jackassery and to move beyond just surviving and into this incredible zone I call thriving.

CLAY CLARK

U.S. Small Business Administration Entrepreneur of the Year and founder of thrive15.com.

CHAPTER 1:
The Basics

Calling Leads = Success

TIP #1:
Call your leads.

"If you cannot sell, your business will go to hell." - Clay Clark is a father of five kids, the organizer, emcee and host of the General Flynn ReAwaken America Tour (www.TimeToFreeAmerica.com), the former "U.S. SBA Entrepreneur of the Year" for the State of Oklahoma, the founder of several multi-million dollar companies, and the host of the *Thrivetime Show* podcast which has been number one overall on the iTunes business podcast charts 6 times. Clay Clark is a member of the *Forbes* Business Coach Council, an Amazon best-selling author, and the host of the *Thrivetime Show* podcast which has hit #1 on the iTunes charts in the category of business 6 times. Throughout his career he's co-founded/founded several multi-million dollar businesses including:

www.DJConnection.com
www.EpicPhotos.com
www.EITRLounge.com
www.MakeYourLifeEpic.com

Party Perfect (which was purchased by Party Pro Rentals)
TipTopK9 Franchising (Clay Clark did not start TipTopK9 Dog Training, he co-founded TipTopK9 Franchising)
www.Thrive15.com (The interactive online entrepreneurship school)
The Tulsa Bridal Association Wedding Show

"I have always said that everyone is in sales. Maybe you don't hold the title of salesperson, but if the business you are in requires you to deal with people, you my friend, are in sales."

- Zig Ziglar
(American author, salesman, and motivational speaker.)

"Half the battle is selling music, not singing it. It's the image, not what you sing."

- Rod Stewart
(Sir Roderick David Stewart CBE (born January 10, 1945) is a British rock and pop singer and songwriter. Born and raised in London, he is of Scottish and English ancestry. With his distinctive raspy singing voice, Stewart is among the best-selling music artists of all time, having sold more than 120 million records worldwide. He has had 10 number-one albums and 31 top-ten singles in the UK, six of which reached number one. Stewart has had 16 top-ten singles in the US, with four reaching number one on the Billboard Hot 100. He was knighted in the 2016 Birthday Honours for services to music and charity.)

TIP #2:

After you call your lead, text your lead and then call your lead again.

TIP #3:

Maybe your prospect has a phone that has been turned off, so text and call your lead again.

TIP #4:

Maybe the person you are calling is in the bathroom, so wait 30 seconds and then call the lead again and knock on the bathroom door.

TIP #5:

Email your leads, and then call them.

TIP #6:

After emailing your lead, call, text, and email your lead until they cry, buy, or die.

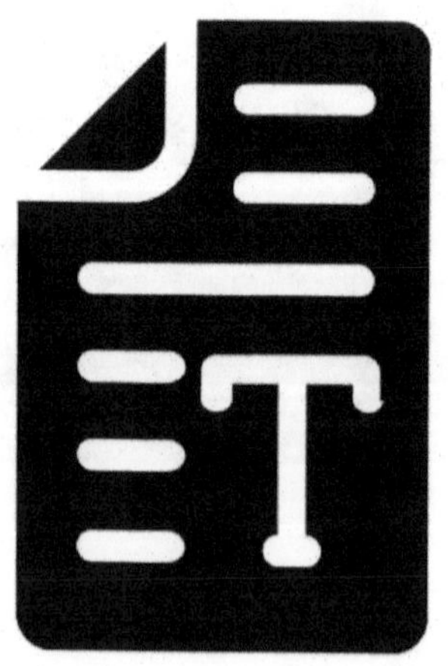

No Script = No Sales

TIP #7:

1% training.
99% reminding.
Call your leads.
Just do it. This is
me reminding you.

TIP #8:

Quit talking, go call your leads.

TIP #9:

Few people like calling their leads. Everyone likes money. With that being said, call your leads.

FUN FACT

"Buyers said that only 20% of sales people add value to the transaction. On the positive side, sales reps who were able to add value saw five times greater engagement with their potential buyers."

- www.salesforce.com

TIP #10:

When's your next appointment?

Until then, go call your leads.

TIP #11:

Don't have any appointments? Sip on a nice warm glass of shut-the-hell-up and then call your leads.

You should have been calling your leads. Go call your leads.

FUN FACT

"4% percent of the salespeople in the U.S. sell 94% of the goods and services."

- Harvard University and Gallup

TIP #12:

The path to financial freedom is to call your leads.

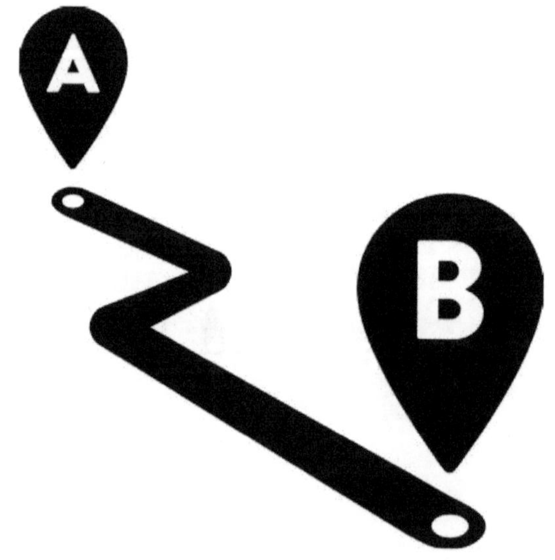

TIP #13:

Looking for a promotion?

Go call your leads until your finger bleeds from dialing and smiling until you call them all.

FUN FACT

100% of the leads that you don't call will not be called.

TIP #14:
What should you do now?

Be strategic and call your leads.

TIP #15:

"I think we should have a meeting about... Nevermind, call your leads."

If you don't have a clarityvoice.com or a call recording service you should be nervous about what your people are saying to your leads that could be paying.

TIP #16:
Dial and smile. Call your leads.

TIP #17:
Right before you do anything else, call your leads.

"You don't have to be a genius or a visionary or even a college graduate to be successful. You just need a framework and a dream."

- Michael Dell
(Founder and CEO of Dell Technologies (he called his leads.)

TIP #18:
Want a raise?
Call your leads.

"I don't think anyone deserves a raise just for showing up... If you've been at a company for three years, then expect a raise in the fourth year, why? If you want consistent raises, you have to keep learning and adding to your skillset all the time."
- BusinessInsider.com

"You don't get paid for the hour. You get paid for the value you bring to the hour.
- Jim Rohn
(Legendary self-help author and sales trainer.)

TIP #19:
Suffering from Erectile Dysfunction?

Having problems with your love life? Call your leads.

"Adults now spend 11 hours per day listening to, watching, reading, or generally interacting with media (and not calling their leads)."

- Nielsen 2018

TIP #20:

I've got a severe fever, and the only prescription is to call your leads.

TIP #21:

Yesterday is history, tomorrow is a mystery. Call your leads today or live a life of misery.

One Day at A Time

TIP #22:

Leads are a lot like significant others. They will leave you if you never talk to them.

TIP #23:

Call your leads, or somebody else will.

TIP #24:

When you feel like you're out of things to do, call your leads.

TIP #25:

If you don't call, text, and email your leads they won't be called, texted, or emailed.

TIP #26:

Call your leads if you want to own planes. Don't call your leads if you want financial pain.

"If thousest doth not calleth thy leads, thou leads will not be calledeth."

- Someone who sold alot of things by calling their leads

TIP #27:

You can do it. Call your leads. And you if you can't do it, still call your leads.

"People who are unable to motivate themselves must be content with mediocrity, no matter how impressive their other talents."

- Andrew Carnegie

(One of the richest people and Americans ever.)

TIP #28:

Call your leads, text your leads, email your leads, Facebook message, send a SnapChat message to your leads, send an Instagram direct message to your leads, send a TikTok message to your leads, send a Truth Social message to your leads, send a Twitter private message, send a Youtube message, send a Telegram message to your leads, and do whatever you have to do to reach your leads.

TIP #29:

In a post-apocalyptic world, send smoke signals to your leads, and then strap tiny messages to the backs of cockroaches so that they can reach your leads.

TIP #30:
Smile and dial. Call your leads.

#noexcuses

TIP #31:
Be encouraged. Call your leads. If you are discouraged, call your leads.

"The way to develop self-confidence is to do the thing you fear and get a record of successful experiences behind you."

- William Jennings Bryan

(American orator and politician, 3-time Democratic Party nominee for President of the United States.)

TIP #32:

If you are gay or if you are straight, call your leads unless you don't want food on your plate.

"With 24/7 connectivity, we face a growing time famine, where the pressure to get work done may eclipse the desire to socialize."
- www.nytimes.com

TIP #33:

If you just got hung up on, call your leads.

Stay Focused

1. Some Will
2. Some Won't
3. So What?
4. What's Next?!

TIP #34:

Looking to take a sick day? Even if you don't feel well, call your leads.

FUN FACT

"If you called in sick to work during the last year even though you felt fine, you're not alone. Thirty eight percent of U.S. employees did it - using such lame excuses as being stuck under a bed - according to an annual survey by CareerBuilder, the largest online job site in the U.S."

- www.usatoday.com

TIP #35:

The fastest path to driving a Bentley is by calling your leads.

TIP #36:

We have no historical proof that President Abraham Lincoln didn't say, "Call your leads".

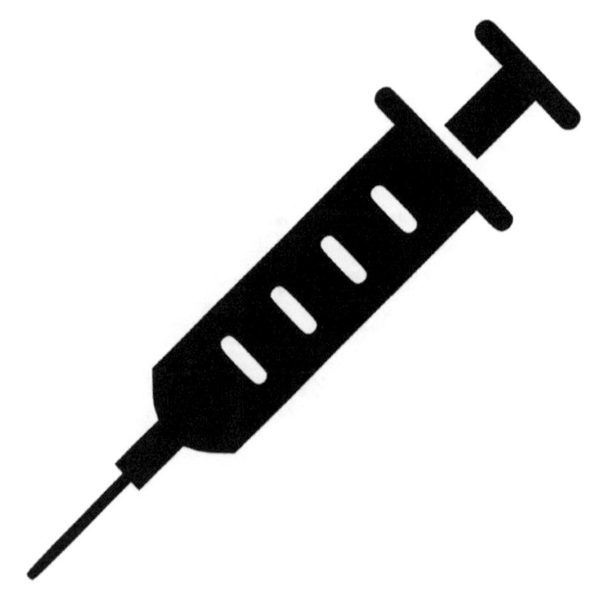

TIP #37:

Want to build a business? Then you need to call your leads.

TIP #38:

No time? Make time to call your leads.

TIP #39:

The trick to hitting your sales quota is to call your leads.

FUN FACT

"Your sales team has a 56% greater chance to attain quota if you engage buyers before they contact a seller."

- blog.hubspot.com

TIP #40:
Don't feel like calling your leads? Call your leads.

"You can't get much done in life if you only work on the days when you feel good."

- Jerry "The Logo" West

(Retired NBA Hall of Fame Basketball Player.)

TIP #41:

The hardest part about calling your leads is starting to call your leads.

"The secret of getting ahead is getting started."

- Mark Twain

(American writer, humorist, entrepreneur, publisher, and lecturer.}

TIP #42:

Before the end of the day, call your leads.

TIP #43:

Come hell or high water, call your leads.

TIP #44:

The most important rule in sales is to call your leads.

TIP #45:

Call your leads.
Wait three seconds
to pause and reflect
on your life and
then call your
leads again.

TIP #46:
Want more time freedom? Call your leads.

TIP #47:

Having a bad day? The best remedy is to call your leads.

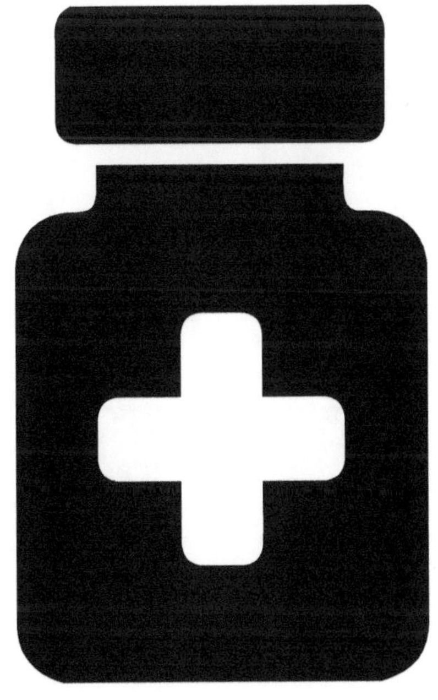

TIP #48:

Less Twitter. More "call your leads".

TIP #49:

We have no proof that President George Washington didn't say, "Men, shut-up and call your leads."

"It takes 18 dials to connect with a single buyer."

- blog.hubspot.com-blog.hubspot.com

TIP #50:

It's the holidays! Celebrate by calling your leads.

FUN FACT

Steve Currington bought this plane as a result of calling his leads.

YOUNG GRASSHOPPER, CALL YOUR LEADS SLOW. POVERTY COMES QUICKLY.

CHAPTER 2:
Expert Tips

TIP #51:

The meaning of life is to call your leads.

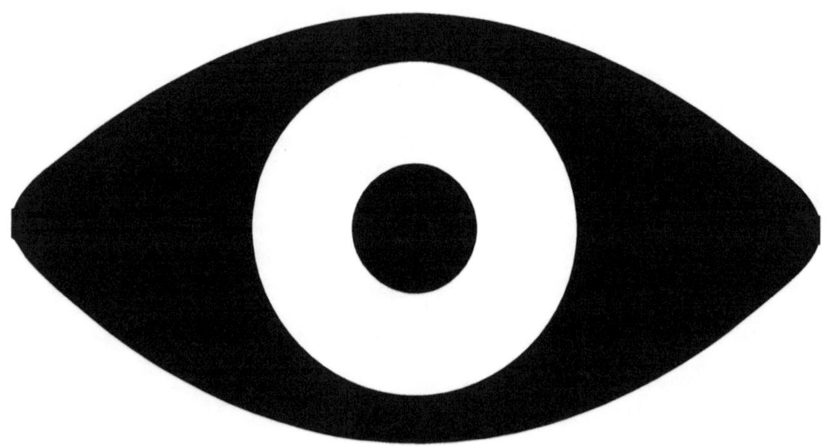

TIP #52:

On the day before Thanksgiving, call your leads.

It's not illegal to call your leads before the holidays, during the holidays, or after the holidays.

TIP #53:

On Thanksgiving calls your leads.

TIP #54:

On Christmas Eve, share the holiday spirit by calling your leads.

FUN FACT

"Less than 25% of companies who receive web leads will respond by phone."
- blog.hubspot.com

TIP #55:

Do you think that you may have called the same leads too much? Call your leads to find out.

"Without continual growth and progress, such words as improvement, achievement, and success have no meaning."

- Benjamin Franklin

(One of the Founding Fathers of the United States.)

TIP #56:

The secret to success is to call your leads.

FUN FACT

Steve Currington and his mom posed for this photo in front of Steve's plane after discussing the importance of calling their leads.

TIP #57:
This just in: call your leads.

TIP #58:

Is it too early in the morning to call your leads? Call your leads to discover if it's too early to call your leads.

QUOTE

"The point is this: whoever sows sparingly will also reap sparingly, and whoever sows bountifully will also reap bountifully."

- 2 Corinthians 9:6

TIP #59:

Is it too late to call your leads?
Call your leads late into the night to find out.

TIP #60:

Do your job:
Call your leads.

TIP #61:
Live long and prosper... and call your leads.

TIP #62:

Be kind. Rewind. And then call your leads.

TIP #63:

Get on the phone and call your leads.

TIP #64:

Turn your leads into deals by calling your leads even while sitting down to eat meals.

TIP #65:
Did they block your phone number? Pick up another phone and call your leads.

"There is no prize in sales for second place. It's win or nothing. The masters know this and strive for - they fight for- that winning edge."

- Jeffrey Gitomer

(American author, professional speaker, and business trainer.)

TIP #66:

Want to become better at sales? Call your leads.

FACT

Steve Currington bought this Lamborghini after calling his leads.

TIP #67:
The key to sales is to call your leads.

#itsnotrocketscience

TIP #68:

Beat your competition to the office to call your leads.

TIP #69:

Stop talking. Get on the phone. Call your leads.

"The way to get started is to quit talking and begin doing."

- Walt Disney

(Founder of Walt Disney World Resorts & pioneer of the American animation industry.)

TIP #70:

Did your client miss an appointment? Call your leads.

TIP #71:

Have an extra 5 minutes? Call your leads.

TIP #72:

Don't be surprised when I say, "call your leads".

Pro-tip: Call your D#@N Leads.

TIP #73:

You miss 100 percent of the appointments you don't set.
Call your leads.

"Winners are not afraid of losing. But losers are. Failure is part of the process of success. People who avoid failure also avoid success."

- Robert T. Kiyosaki

(Author of *Rich Dad Poor Dad* (#1 personal finance book of all time.)

TIP #74:

Insanity is trusting your staff to call your leads. Follow up, follow up, and follow up until they call their leads.

TIP #75:

Dream big.

Call your leads and drive Lamborghinis.

TIP #76:

Don't wait until you are motivated.

Call your leads.

"Nothing is impossible. 'Impossible' just takes a few more phone calls."

- Michael J. Fox

(Canadian-American actor, author, producer, and activist.)

TIP #77:

Quit thinking about your feelings and call your leads.

"If you're going through hell, keep going."

- Winston Churchill

(Prime Minister of the United Kingdom who stood up against Adolf Hitler and the Nazi party during World War II.)

TIP #78:

Hey you. Yeah, you. Call your leads.

TIP #79:

Snap!

Crackle!

Pop!

Call your Leads and do not stop!

QUOTE

"The top salesperson in the organization probably missed more sales than 90% of the sales people on the team, but they also made more calls than the others made."

- Zig Ziglar

(American Author, salesman, and motivational speaker.)

TIP #80:

When it rains, it pours. When you call your leads, you make more.

TIP #81:

Not calling your leads is the first sign of "Jackassary" taking root in your life.

"Sales are contingent upon the attitude of the salesman - not the attitude of the prospect."

- W. Clement Stone

(Businessman, philanthropist and New Thought self-help book author.)

TIP #82:

Just got divorced? Call your leads.

TIP #83:
Just got engaged? Call your leads.

TIP #84:

Just got yelled at by a prospect? Call your leads.

TIP #85:

Does your husband work for you? Will your husband not call his leads?

Fire your husband and call your leads.

"One in 4 workers admitted that, during a typical workday, they will spend at least an hour on personal calls, emails, or texts."

- www.career.builder.com

TIP #86:
Quit looking at your phone waiting for inbound sales calls. Call your d@#n leads!

"The early bird gets the worm. 50% of sales go to the first salesperson to contact the prospect."

- www.InsideSales.com

TIP #87:
ABC - Always be calling your leads.

FUN FACT

"80% of sales require 5 follow-up calls after the meeting. 44% of salespeople give up after 1 follow-up."

- www.marketingdonut.co.uk.com

TIP #88:

Looking for the secret to holiday happiness with your extended family?

Step outside and call your leads.

TIP #89:

Want to drive a Lamborghini and your kids to not be skinny? Call your leads and stop pinching pennies.

QUOTE

"Obstacles are necessary for success because in selling, as in all careers of importance, victory comes only after many struggles and countless defeats."

- Og Mandino

(Author of the *The Greatest Salesman in the World.*)

TIP #90:

Call your leads until you hate yourself and then call your leads.

"In 2007 it took an average of 3.68 cold call attempts to reach a prospect. Today it takes 8 attempts."

- www.ovationsales.com

TIP #91:

Quit sorting your leads and start calling your leads.

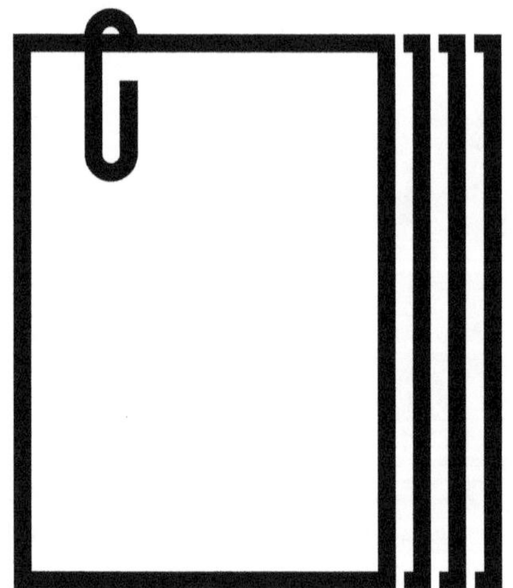

"The average salesperson only makes 2 attempts to reach a prospect."

- www.siriusdecisions.com

TIP #92:

Stop getting coffees, sorting your emails, and going to the bathroom.

Call your leads.

TIP #93:

No one cares about your leads... only you do. So call your leads.

"Nobody cares how much you know, until they know how much you care."

-Theodore Roosevelt

(26th president of the United States and certified badass.)

TIP #94:

Turn off your notifications. It will help you call your leads.

TIP #95:

You will not find time to call your leads. Just call your leads.

Here is a clock - time is already found.

TIP #96:

This is a Lamborghini you will never be able to afford unless you call your leads.

FUN FACT

"Beds are for the weak. I sleep standing up so I can call my leads."

- Steve Currington

(Owner of GetKoalified.com and proud owner of a Lamborghini.)

TIP #97:

Looking for a spiritual change in your life?
Call your leads.

TIP #98:

Make sure you have it in your calendar this week to call your leads.

"Vision without execution is hallucination."

- Thomas Edison

(American inventor and businessman, who has been described as America's greatest inventor.)

TIP #99:

Block off time in your sales team's calendar to call their leads.

"As I grow older, I pay less attention to what men say, I just watch what they do."

- Andrew Carnegie

(One of the richest people and Americans ever.)

TIP #100:

Can't sleep? Take some Nyquil, then in the morning wake up and call your leads.

"If you really want to do something, you'll find a way. If you don't, you'll find an excuse."

-Jim Rohn

(American entrepreneur, author, and motivational speaker.)

TIP #101:
Call your leads, call your leads and for the love of all that is good, call your leads and quit not calling your leads.

QUOTE

"Success isn't a result of spontaneous combustion. You must set yourself on fire."

- Arnold H. Glasgow
(America business man who ran a humor magazine for 60 years.)

"Knowledge without implementation is meaningless."

- Napoleon Hill
(The best-selling author of *Think & Grow Rich* and a man who called his leads.)

WANT TO KNOW EVEN MORE?
CHECK OUT ALL OF CLAY'S BOOKS

START HERE
The World's Best Business Growth & Consulting Book: Business Growth Strategies from the World's Best Business Coach.

DON'T LET YOUR EMPLOYEES HOLD YOU HOSTAGE
This candid book shares how to avoid being held hostage by employees.

MAKE YOUR LIFE EPIC
Clay shares his journey and struggle from the dorm room to the board room during his raw and action-packed story of how he built DJConnection.com.

THE ENTREPRENEUR'S DRAGON ENERGY
The Mindset Kanye, Trump and You Need to Succeed.

BOOM
The 14 Proven Steps to Business Success.

F6 JOURNAL
Meta Thrive Time Journal.

JACKASSARY
Jackassery will serve as a beacon of light for other entrepreneurs that are looking to avoid troublesome employees and difficult situations. This is real. This is raw. This is unfiltered entrepreneurship.

THE ART OF GETTING THINGS DONE
Clay Clark breaks down the proven, time-tested and time freedom creating super moves that you can use to create both the time freedom and financial freedom that most people only dream about.

HOW TO REPEL FRIENDS AND NOT INFLUENCE PEOPLE
The epic whale of a tale featuring America's self proclaimed most humble male.

THRIVE
How to Take Control of Your Destiny and Move Beyond Surviving... Now!

SEARCH ENGINE DOMINATION
Learn the Proven System We've Used to Earn Millions.

SALES DOMINATION
Clay Clark is a master of selling and now he wants to teach you his proven processes, scalable systems and sales mastery moves in a humorous and practical way.

WHEEL OF WEALTH
An Entrepreneur's Action Guide.

WILL NOT WORK FOR FOOD
9 Big Ideas for Effectively Managing Your Business in an Increasingly Dumb, Distracted & Dishonest America.

TRADE-UPS
Learn how to design and live the life you love, how to find and create the time needed to get things done in a world filled with endless digital distractions, and more!

IF MY WALLS COULD TALK
The Notes, Quotes, & Epiphanies I've Written On Clay's Office Walls. (Hardcover).

IT'S NOT LONELY AT THE TOP
15 Keys to achieving a successful, peaceful, and drama-free life. (3/4 of this book is handwritten by Clay Clark, himself).

PODCAST DOMINATION 101
This book will show you how to prepare, record, launch, and begin generating income from your podcast, all from your home studio!

ENTREPRENEURSHIP: SIMPLIFIED, AMPLIFIED, & VISUALIZED
Throughout my career, I have been blessed to achieve tremendous success both as an entrepreneur and as a podcast host.

THE GREAT RESET VERSUS THE GREAT AWAKENING
The Great Reset Versus The Great Awakening breaks down this EPIC battle between good and evil.

FEAR UNMASKED
Fear Unmasked gives you the essential information you need to know about the coronavirus, the government shutdown, and the media that is perpetuating the hysteria.

FEAR UNMASKED 2.0
Updated and revised for 2021. Fear Unmasked 2.0 provides more resources to kill the spirit of fear and giving YOU an action plan to save America.

Steve Currington bought this Lamborghini by calling his leads.

I MADE COPIOUS AMOUNTS OF
MONEY CALLING MY LEADS.

- STEVE CURRINGTON

THIS STEERING WHEEL WAS PAID
FOR BY CALLING MY LEADS.

- STEVE CURRINGTON

FUN FACT

This wheel is found on a Lamborghini
that Steve Currington bought this
calling his leads.

Bonus Tip:

Looking for the ultimate sales lead management and customer relationship software?

You will find it by calling your leads until your dialing finger bleeds.

www.ingramcontent.com/pod-product-compliance
Lightning Source LLC
Chambersburg PA
CBHW041335120726
48005CB00014B/2264